This Book Belongs To:

____

Made in the USA
Columbia, SC
28 September 2023

23545532R00074